Dreams & dust, poems

Don Marquis

& DUST

POEMS

BY

DON MARQUIS

HARPER & BROTHERS PUBLISHERS
NEW YORK & LONDON

DREAMS AND DUST

Printed in the United States of America
Published October, 1915

G-P

TO

MY MOTHER

VIRGINIA WHITMORE MARQUIS

CONTENTS

CONTENTS

SHADOWS

COLORS AND SURFACES

DREAMS AND DUST

CONTENTS

LYRICS

CONTENTS

REALITIES

PROEM

"SO LET THEM PASS, THESE SONGS OF MINE"

So let them pass, these songs of mine,
Into oblivion, nor repine;
Abandoned ruins of large schemes,
Dimmed lights adrift from nobler dreams,

Weak wings I sped on quests divine,
So let them pass, these songs of mine.
They soar, or sink ephemeral—
I care not greatly which befall!

For if no song I e'er had wrought,
Still have I loved and laughed and fought;
So let them pass, these songs of mine;
I sting too hot with life to whine!

Still shall I struggle, fail, aspire,
Lose God, and find Gods in the mire,
And drink dream-deep life's heady wine—
So let them pass, these songs of mine.

DAYLIGHT HUMORS

THIS IS ANOTHER DAY

I AM mine own priest, and I shrive myself
Of all my wasted yesterdays. Though sin
And sloth and foolishness, and all ill weeds
Of error, evil, and neglect grow rank
And ugly there, I dare forgive myself
That error, sin, and sloth and foolishness.
God knows that yesterday I played the fool;
God knows that yesterday I played the knave;
But shall I therefore cloud this new dawn o'er
With fog of futile sighs and vain regrets?

This is another day! And flushed Hope walks
Adown the sunward slopes with golden shoon.
This is another day; and its young strength
Is laid upon the quivering hills until,
Like Egypt's Memnon, they grow quick with song.
This is another day, and the bold world
Leaps up and grasps its light, and laughs, as leapt
Prometheus up and wrenched the fire from Zeus.

This is another day—are its eyes blurred
With maudlin grief for any wasted past?
A thousand thousand failures shall not daunt!
Let dust clasp dust; death, death—I am alive!
And out of all the dust and death of mine
Old selves I dare to lift a singing heart
And living faith; my spirit dares drink deep
Of the red mirth mantling in the cup of morn.

APRIL SONG

FLEET across the grasses
  Flash the feet of Spring,
Piping, as he passes
Fleet across the grasses,
"Follow, lads and lasses!
  Sing, world, sing!"
Fleet across the grasses
  Flash the feet of Spring!

Idle winds deliver
  Rumors through the town,
Tales of reeds that quiver,
Idle winds deliver,
Where the rapid river
  Drags the willows down—
Idle winds deliver
  Rumors through the town.

In the country places
  By the silver brooks
April airs her graces;
In the country places
Wayward April paces,
  Laughter in her looks;
In the country places
  By the silver brooks.

Hints of alien glamor
  Even reach the town;
Urban muses stammer
Hints of alien glamor,
But the city's clamor
  Beats the voices down;
Hints of alien glamor
  Even reach the town.

THIS EARTH, IT IS ALSO A STAR

WHERE the singers of Saturn find tongue,
  Where the Galaxy's lovers embrace,
Our world and its beauty are sung!
  They lean from their casements to trace
  If our planet still spins in its place;
Faith fables the thing that we are,
  And Fantasy laughs and gives chase:
This earth, it is also a star!

Round the sun, that is fixèd, and hung
  For a lamp in the darkness of space
We are whirled, we are swirled, we are flung;
  Singing and shining we race
  And our light on the uplifted face
Of dreamer or prophet afar
  May fall as a symbol of grace:
This earth, it is also a star!

Looking out where our planet is swung
  Doubt loses his writhen grimace,
Dry hearts drink the gleams and are young;—
  Where agony's boughs interlace
  His Garden some Jesus may pace,
Lifting, the wan avatar,
  His soul to this light as a vase!
This earth, it is also a star!

Great spirits in sorrowful case
  Yearn to us through the vapors that bar:
Canst think of that, soul, and be base?—
  This earth, it is also a star!

THE NAME

It shifts and shifts from form to form,
  It drifts and darkles, gleams and glows;
It is the passion of the storm,
  The poignance of the rose;
Through changing shapes, through devious
        ways,
  By noon or night, through cloud or flame,
My heart has followed all my days
  Something I cannot name.

In sunlight on some woman's hair,
  Or starlight in some woman's eyne,
Or in low laughter smothered where
  Her red lips wedded mine,
My heart hath known, and thrilled to know,
  This unnamed presence that it sought;
And when my heart hath found it so,
  "*Love is the name,*" I thought.

Sometimes when sudden afterglows
  In futile glory storm the skies
Within their transient gold and rose
  The secret stirs and dies;
Or when the trampling morn walks o'er
  The troubled seas, with feet of flame,
My awed heart whispers, "*Ask no more,*
  For Beauty is the name!"

Or dreaming in old chapels where
  The dim aisles pulse with murmurings
That part are music, part are prayer—
  (Or rush of hidden wings)
Sometimes I lift a startled head
  To some saint's carven countenance,
Half fancying that the lips have said,
  "*All names mean God, perchance!*"

THE BIRTH

There is a legend that the love of God
So quickened under Mary's heart it wrought
Her very maidenhood to holier stuff. . . .
However that may be, the birth befell
Upon a night when all the Syrian stars
Swayed tremulous before one lordlier orb
That rose in gradual splendor,
Paused,
Flooding the firmament with mystic light,
And dropped upon the breathing hills
A sudden music
Like a distillation from its gleams;
A rain of spirit and a dew of song!

A MOOD OF PAVLOWA

The soul of the Spring through its body of earth
  Bursts in a bloom of fire,
And the crocuses come in a rainbow riot of mirth....
  They flutter, they burn, they take wing, they
    aspire. . . .
Wings, motion and music and flame,
Flower, woman and laughter, and all these the
    same!
She is light and first love and the youth of the
    world,
She is sandaled with joy . . . she is lifted and
    whirled,
She is flung, she is swirled, she is driven along
  By the carnival winds that have torn her away
  From the coronal bloom on the brow of the
    May. . . .
She is youth, she is foam, she is flame, she is
    visible Song!

THE POOL

Reach over, my Undine, and clutch me a reed—
Nymph of mine idleness, notch me a pipe—
For I am fulfilled of the silence, and long
For to utter the sense of the silence in song.

Down-stream all the rapids are troubled with pebbles
That fetter and fret what the water would utter,
And it rushes and splashes in tremulous trebles;
It makes haste through the shallows, its soul is aflutter;

But here all the sound is serene and outspread
In the murmurous moods of a slow-swirling pool;
Here all the sounds are unhurried and cool;
Every silence is kith to a sound; they are wed,
They are mated, are mingled, are tangled, are bound;
Every hush is in love with a sound, every sound
By the law of its life to some silence is bound.

Then here will we hide; idle here and abide,
In the covert here, close by the waterside—
Here, where the slim flattered reeds are aquiver
With the exquisite hints of the reticent river,
  Here, where the lips of this pool are the lips
Of all pools, let us listen and question and wait;
  Let us hark to the whispers of love and of death,
Let us hark to the lispings of life and of fate—
In this place where pale silences flower into sound
Let us strive for some secret of all the profound
Deep and calm Silence that meshes men 'round!
There's as much of God hinted in one ripple's
    plashes—
  There's as much of Truth glints in yon dragon-
    fly's flight—
There's as much Purpose gleams where yonder
    trout flashes
  As in—any book else!—could we read things
    aright.

Then nymph of mine indolence, here let us hide,
Learn, listen, and question; idle here and abide
Where the rushes and lilies lean low to the tide.

"THEY HAD NO POET . . ."

"Vain was the chief's, the sage's pride!
They had no poet and they died."—Pope.

By Tigris, or the streams of Ind,
Ere Colchis rose, or Babylon,
Forgotten empires dreamed and sinned,
Setting tall towns against the dawn,

Which, when the proud Sun smote upon,
Flashed fire for fire and pride for pride;
Their names were . . . Ask oblivion! . . .
"They had no poet, and they died."

Queens, dusk of hair and tawny-skinned,
That loll where fellow leopards fawn . . .
Their hearts are dust before the wind,
Their loves, that shook the world, are wan!

Passion is mighty . . . but, anon,
Strong Death has Romance for his bride;

Their legends . . . Ask oblivion! . . .
"They had no poet, and they died."

Heroes, the braggart trumps that dinned
Their futile triumphs, monarch, pawn,
Wild tribesmen, kingdoms disciplined,
Passed like a whirlwind and were gone;

They built with bronze and gold and brawn,
The inner Vision still denied;
Their conquests . . . Ask oblivion! . . .
"They had no poet, and they died."

Dumb oracles, and priests withdrawn,
Was it but flesh they deified?
Their gods were . . . Ask oblivion! . . .
"They had no poet, and they died."

NEW YORK

SHE is hot to the sea that crouches beside,
  Human and hot to the cool stars peering down,
  My passionate city, my quivering town,
And her dark blood, tide upon purple tide,
With throbs as of thunder beats,
  With leaping rhythms and vast, is swirled
Through the shaken lengths of her veinèd streets . . .
  She pulses, the heart of a world!

I have thrilled with her ecstasy, agony, woe—
Hath she a mood that I do not know?
The winds of her music tumultuous have seized
        me and swayed me,
  Have lifted, have swung me around
  In their whorls as of cyclonic sound;
Her passions have torn me and tossed me and
        brayed me;
Drunken and trancèd and dazzled with visions
        and gleams,

I have spun with her dervish priests;
I have searched to the souls of her hunted beasts
And found love sleeping there;
I have soared on the wings of her flashing dreams;
I have sunk with her dull despair;
I have sweat with her travails and cursed with her pains;
I have swelled with her foolish pride;
I have raged through a thick red mist at one with her branded Cains,
With her broken Christs have died.

O beautiful half-god city of visions and love!
O hideous half-brute city of hate!
O wholly human and baffled and passionate town!
The throes of thy burgeoning, stress of thy fight,
Thy bitter, blind struggle to gain for thy body a soul,
I have known, I have felt, and been shaken thereby!
Wakened and shaken and broken,
For I hear in thy thunders terrific that throb through thy rapid veins
The beat of the heart of a world.

A HYMN

(1914)

Clothed on with thunder and with steel
  And black against the dawn
The whirling armies clash and reel. . . .
  A wind, and they are gone
  Like mists withdrawn,
  Like mists withdrawn!

Like clouds withdrawn, like driven sands,
  Earth's body vanisheth:
One solid thing unconquered stands,
  The ghost that humbles death.
  All else is breath,
  All else is breath!

Man rose from out the stinging slime,
  Half brute, and sought a soul,
And up the starrier ways of time,
  Half god, unto his goal,

What though worlds stagger, and the suns
  Seem shaken in their place,
Trust thou the leaping love that runs
  Creative over space:
  Take heart of grace,
  Take heart of grace!

What though great kingdoms fall on death
  Before the stabbing blade,
Their brazen might was only breath,
  Their substance but a shade—
  Be not dismayed,
  Be not dismayed!

Man's dream which conquered brute and clod
  Shall fail not, but endure,
Shall rise, though beaten to the sod,
  Shall hold its vantage sure—
  As sure as God,
  As sure as God!

THE SINGER

LITTLE while, with love and youth,
He wandered, singing:—
  He felt life's pulses hot and strong
  Beat all his rapid veins along;
  He wrought life's rhythms into song:
    He laughed, he sang the Dawn!
  So close, so close to life he dwelt
  That at rare times and rapt he felt
  The fleshly barriers yield and melt;
    He trembled, looking on
  Creation at her miracles;
  His soul-sight pierced the earthly shells
  And saw the spirit weave its spells,
    The veil of clay withdrawn;—
little while, with love and youth,
He wandered, singing!

little while, with age and death,
He wanders, dreaming;—

No more the thunder and the urge
Of earth's full tides that storm the verge
Of heaven with their sweep and surge
  Shall lift, shall bear him on;
Where is the golden hope that led
Him comrade with the mighty dead?
The love that aureoled his head?—
  The glory is withdrawn!
How shall one soar with broken wings?
The leaguèd might of futile things
Wars with the heart that dares and sings;—
  It is not always Dawn!
A little while, with age and death,
  He wanders, dreaming.

WORDS ARE NOT GUNS

Put by the sword (a dreamer saith),
  The years of peace draw nigh!
Already the millennial dawn
  Makes red the eastern sky!

Be not deceived. It comes not yet!
  The ancient passions keep
Alive beneath their changing masks.
  They are not dead. They sleep.

Surely peace comes. As sure as Man
  Rose from primeval slime.
That was not yesterday. There's still
  A weary height to climb!

And we can dwell too long with dreams
  And play too much with words,
Forgetting our inheritance
  Was bought and held with swords.

But Truth (you say) *makes tyrants quail—*
Beats down embattled Wrong?
If truth be armed! Be not deceived.
The strife is to the strong.

Words are not guns. Words are not ships.
And ships and guns prevail.
Our liberties, that blood has gained,
Are guarded, or they fail.

Truth does not triumph without blows,
Error not tamely yields.
But falsehood closes with quick faith,
Fierce, on a thousand fields.

And surely, somewhat of that faith
Our fathers fought for clings!
Which called this freedom's hemisphere,
Despite Earth's leaguèd kings.

Great creeds grow thews, or else they die.
Thought clothed in deed is lord.
What are thy gods? Thy gods brought love?
They also brought a sword.

Unchallenged, shall we always stand,
Secure, apart, aloof?
Be not deceived. That hour shall come
Which puts us to the proof.

Then, that we hold the trust we have
Safeguarded for our sons,
Let us cease dreaming! Let us have
More ships, more troops, more guns!

WITH THE SUBMARINES

Above, the baffled twilight fails; beneath, the
blind snakes creep;
Beside us glides the chainel shark, our pilot
through the deep;
And, lurking where low headlands shield from
cruising scout and spy,
We bide the signal through the gloom that bids
us slay or die.

All watchful, mute, the crouching guns that guard
the strait sea lanes—
Watchful and hawklike, plumed with hate, the
desperate aeroplanes—
And still as death and swift as fate, above the
darkling coasts,
The spying Wireless sows the night with troops
of stealthy ghosts,

While hushed through all her huddled streets the
tide-walled city waits
The drumming thunders that announce brute
battle at her gates.

Southward a hundred windy leagues, through
storms that blind and bar,
Our cheated cruisers search the waves, our cap-
tains seek the war;
But here the port of peril is; the foeman's dread-
noughts ride
Sullen and black against the moon, upon a sullen
tide.
And only we to launch ourselves against their
stark advance—
To guide uncertain lightnings through these treach-
erous seas of chance!

. . . . . .

And now a wheeling searchlight paints a signal on
the night;
And now the bellowing guns are loud with the
wild lust of fight.

. . . . . .

And now, her flanks of steel apulse with all the
power of hell,
Forth from the darkness leaps in pride a hateful
miracle,
The flagship of their Admiral—and now God help
and save!—
We challenge Death at Death's own game; we
sink beneath the wave!

. . . . . .

Ah, steady now—and one good blow—one straight
stab through the gloom—
Ah, good!—the thrust went home!—she founders—
flounders to her doom!—
Full speed ahead!—those damned quick-firing guns
—but let them bark—
What's that—the dynamos?—they've got us, men!
—*Christ! in the dark!*

NICHOLAS OF MONTENEGRO

(1912)

He speaks as straight as his rifles shot,
  As straight as a thrusting blade,
Waiting the deed that shall trouble the truce
  His savage guns have made.

"You have dared the wrath of a dozen states,"
  Was the challenge that he heard;
"We can die but once!" said the grim old King
  As he gripped his mountain sword.

"For I paid in blood for the town I took,
  The blood of my brave men slain,—
And if you covet the town I took
  You must buy it with blood again!"

Stern old King of the stark, black hills,
  Where the lean, fierce eagles breed,
Your speech rings true as your good sword rings—
  And you are a king indeed!

DICKENS

"The only book that the party had was a volume of Dickens. During the six months that they lay in the cave which they had hacked in the ice, waiting for spring to come, they read this volume through again and again."—*From a newspaper report of an antarctic expedition.*

HUDDLED within their savage lair
  They hearkened to the prowling wind;
They heard the loud wings of despair . . .
  And madness beat against the mind. . . .
A sunless world stretched stark outside
As if it had cursed God and died;
Dumb plains lay prone beneath the weight
Of cold unutterably great;
  Iron ice bound all the bitter seas,
The brutal hills were bleak as hate. . . .
  Here none but Death might walk at ease!

Then Dickens spoke, and, lo! the vast
  Unpeopled void stirred into life;

The dead world quickened, the mad blast
  Hushed for an hour its idiot strife
With nothingness. . . .

                                        And from the gloom,
  Parting the flaps of frozen skin,
  Old friends and dear came trooping in,
And light and laughter filled the room. . . .
Voices and faces, shapes beloved,
  Babbling lips and kindly eyes,
Not ghosts, but friends that lived and moved .
  They brought the sun from other skies,
They wrought the magic that dispels
  The bitterer part of loneliness . . .
And when they vanished each man dreamed
  His dream there in the wilderness. . . .
One heard the chime of Christmas bells,
And, staring down a country lane,
Saw bright against the window-pane
The firelight beckon warm and red. . . .
And one turned from the waterside
Where Thames rolls down his slothful tide
To breast the human sea that beats
Through roaring London's battered streets

And revel in the moods of men. . . .
  And one saw all the April hills
  Made glad with golden daffodils,
And found and kissed his love again. . . .

. . . . . .

By all the troubled hearts he cheers
  In homely ways or by lost trails,
By all light shed through all dark years
  When hope grows sick and courage quails,
We hail him first among his peers;
  Whether we sorrow, sing, or feast,
He, too, hath known and understood—
  Master of many moods, high priest
Of mirth and lord of cleansing tears!

A POLITICIAN

LEADER no more, be judged of us!
  Hailed Chief, and loved, of yore—
Youth, and the faith of youth, cry out:
  Leader and Chief no more!

We dreamed a Prophet, flushed with faith,
  Content to toil in pain
If that his sacrifice might be,
  Somehow, his people's gain.

We saw a vision, and our blood
  Beat red and hot and strong:
"*Lead us* (we cried) *to war against*
  Some foul, embattled wrong!"

We dreamed a Warrior whose sword
  Was edged for sham and shame;
We dreamed a Statesman far above
  The vulgar lust for fame.

We were not cynics, and we dreamed
  A Man who made no truce
With lies nor ancient privilege
  Nor old, entrenched abuse.

We dreamed . . . we dreamed . . . Youth dreamed a dream!
  And even you forgot
Yourself, one moment, and dreamed, too—
  Struck, while your mood was hot!

Struck three or four good blows . . . and then
  Turned back to easier things:
The cheap applause, the blatant mob,
  The praise of underlings!

Praise . . . praise . . . was ever man so filled,
  So avid still, of praise?
So hungry for the crowd's acclaim,
  The sycophantic phrase?

O you whom Greatness beckoned to . . .
  O swollen Littleness
Who turned from Immortality
  To fawn upon Success!

O blind with love of self, who led
  Youth's vision to defeat,
Bawling and brawling for rewards,
  Loud, in the common street!

O you who were so quick to judge—
  Leader, and loved, of yore—
Hear now the judgment of our youth:
  Leader and Chief no more!

THE BAYONET

(1914)

THE great guns slay from a league away, the death-
bolts fly unseen,
And bellowing hill replies to hill, machine to brute
machine,
But still in the end when the long lines bend and
the battle hangs in doubt
They take to the steel in the same old way that
their fathers fought it out—
It is man to man and breast to breast and eye
to bloodshot eye
And the reach and twist of the thrusting wrist, as
it was in the days gone by!

Along the shaken hills the guns their drumming
thunder roll—
But the keen blades thrill with the lust to kill
that leaps from the slayer's soul!

For hand and heart and living steel, one pulse of
hate they feel.
Is your clan afraid of the naked blade? Does it
flinch from the bitter steel?
Perish your dreams of conquest then, your swollen
hopes and bold,
For empire dwells with the stabbing blade, as it
did in the days of old!

THE BUTCHERS AT PRAYER

(1914)

Each nation as it draws the sword
  And flings its standard to the air
Petitions piously the Lord—
  Vexing the void abyss with prayer.

O irony too deep for mirth!
  O posturing apes that rant, and dare
This antic attitude! O Earth,
  With your wild jest of wicked prayer!

I dare not laugh . . . a rising swell
  Of laughter breaks in shrieks somewhere—
No doubt they relish it in Hell,
  This cosmic jest of Earth at prayer!

SHADOWS

HAUNTED

(THE GHOST SPEAKS)

A GHOST is the freak of a sick man's brain?
  Then why do ye start and shiver so?
That's the sob and drip of a leaky drain?
  But it sounds like another noise we know!
  The heavy drops drummed red and slow,
The drops ran down as slow as fate—
  Do ye hear them still?—it was long ago!—
But here in the shadows I wait, I wait!

Spirits there be that pass in peace;
  Mine passed in a whorl of wrath and dole;
And the hour that your choking breath shall cease
  I will get my grip on your naked soul—
  Nor pity may stay nor prayer cajole—
I would drag ye whining from Hell's own gate:
  To me, to me, ye must pay the toll!
And here in the shadows I wait, I wait!

The dead they are dead, they are out of the way?
  And a ghost is the whim of an ailing mind?
Then why did ye whiten with fear to-day
  When ye heard a voice in the calling wind?
  Why did ye falter and look behind
At the creeping mists when the hour grew late?
  Ye would see my face were ye stricken blind!
And here in the shadows I wait, I wait!

Drink and forget, make merry and boast,
  But the boast rings false and the jest is thin—
In the hour that I meet ye ghost to ghost,
  Stripped of the flesh that ye skulk within,
  Stripped to the coward soul 'ware of its sin,
Ye shall learn, ye shall learn, whether dead men
    hate!
  Ah, a weary time has the waiting been,
But here in the shadows I wait, I wait!

A NIGHTMARE

LEAGUES before me, leagues behind;
  Clamor warring wastes of flood,
All the streams of all the worlds
  Flung together, mad of mood;
Through the cañon beats a sound,
  Regular of interval.
Distant, drumming, muffled, dull,
  Thunderously rhythmical;

Crafts slip by my startled soul—
  Soul that cowers, a thing apart—
They are corpuscles of blood!
  That's the throbbing of a heart!
God of terrors!—am I mad?—
  Through my body, mine own soul,
Shrunken to an atom's size,
  Voyages toward an unguessed goal!

THE MOTHER

THE mother by the gallows-tree,
  The gallows-tree, the gallows-tree,
(While the twitching body mocked the sun)
Lifted to Heaven her broken heart
  And called for sympathy.

Then Mother Mary bent to her,
  Bent from her place by God's left side,
And whispered: "Peace—do I not know?—
  My son was crucified!"

"O Mother Mary," answered she,
  "You cannot, cannot enter in
To my soul's woe—you cannot know—
  For your son wrought no sin!"

(And men whose work compelled them there,
  Their hearts were stricken dead;

They heard the rope creak on the beam;
  I thought I heard the frightened ghost
  Whimpering overhead.)

The mother by the gallows-tree,
  The gallows-tree, the gallows-tree,
Lifted to Christ her broken heart
  And called in agony.

Then Lord Christ bent to her and said:
  "Be comforted, be comforted;
I know your grief; the whole world's woe
  I bore upon my head."

"But O Lord Christ, you cannot know,
  No one can know," she said, "no one"—
(While the quivering corpse swayed in the wind)—
"Lord Christ, no one can understand
  Who never had a son!"

IN THE BAYOU

Lazy and slow, through the snags and trees
  Move the sluggish currents, half asleep;
Around and between the cypress knees,
  Like black, slow snakes the dark tides creep—
How deep is the bayou beneath the trees?
"Knee-deep,
          Knee-deep,
                    Knee-deep,
                              Knee-deep!"
Croaks the big bullfrog of Reelfoot Lake
From his hiding-place in the draggled brake.

What is the secret the slim reeds know
That makes them to shake and to shiver so,
And the scared flags quiver from plume to foot?—
The frogs pipe solemnly, deep and slow:
"Look under
          the root!
                    Look under
                              the root!"

The hoarse frog croaks and the stark owl hoots
Of a mystery moored in the cypress roots.

Was it love turned hate? Was it friend turned foe?
Only the frogs and the gray owl know,
  For the white moon shrouded her face in a mist
At the spurt of a pistol, red and bright—
At the sound of a shriek that stabbed the night—
  And the little reeds were frightened and whist;
But always the eddies whimper and choke,
And the frogs would tell if they could, for they
    croak:
"Deep, deep!
        Death-deep!
                Deep, deep!
                        Death-deep!"
And the dark tide slides and glisters and glides
Snakelike over the secret it hides.

THE SAILOR'S WIFE SPEAKS

Ye are dead, they say, but ye swore, ye swore,
  Ye would come to me back from the sea!
From out of the sea and the night, ye cried,
Nor the crawling weed nor the dragging tide
  Could hold ye fast from me:—
  Come, ah, come to me!

Three spells I have laid on the rising sun
  And three on the waning moon—
Are ye held in the bonds of the night or the day?
Ye must loosen your bonds and away, away!
  Ye must come where I wait ye, soon—
  Ah, soon! soon! soon!

Three times I have cast my words to the wind,
  And thrice to the climbing sea;
If ye drift or dream with the clouds or foam
Ye must drift again home, ye must drift again
      home—

Wraith, ye are free, ye are free;
Ghost, ye are free, ye are free!

Are the coasts of death so fair, so fair?
But I wait ye here on the shore!
It is I that ye hear in the calling wind—
I have stared through the dark till my soul is blind!
O lover of mine, ye swore,
Lover of mine, ye swore!

HUNTED

Oh, why do they hunt so hard, so hard, who have
no need of food?
Do they hunt for sport, do they hunt for hate, do
they hunt for the lust of blood?

. . . . . .

If I were a god I would get me a spear, I would
get me horse and dog,
And merrily, merrily I would ride through covert
and brake and bog,

With hound and horn and laughter loud, over the
hills and away—
For there is no sport like that of a god with a
man that stands at bay!

Ho! but the morning is fresh and fair, and oh!
but the sun is bright,
And yonder the quarry breaks from the brush and
heads for the hills in flight;

A minute's law for the harried thing—then follow
him, follow him fast,
With the bellow of dogs and the beat of hoofs
and the mellow bugle's blast.

. . . . . .

*Hillo! Halloo! they have marked a man! there is
sport in the world to-day—*
*And a clamor swells from the heart of the wood that
tells of a soul at bay!*

A DREAM CHILD

WHERE tides of tossed wistaria bloom
  Foam up in purple turbulence,
Where twining boughs have built a room
  And wing'd winds pause to garner scents
And scattered sunlight flecks the gloom,
  She broods in pensive indolence.

What is the thought that holds her thrall,
  That dims her sight with unshed tears?
What songs of sorrow droop and fall
  In broken music for her ears?
What voices thrill her and recall
  The poignant joy of happier years?

She dreams 'tis not the winds which pass
  That whisper through the shaken vine;
Whose footstep stirs the rustling grass
  None else that listened might divine;
She sees her child that never was
  Look up with longing in his eyne.

Unkissed, his lifted forehead gains
  A grace not earthly, but more rare—
For since her heart but only feigns,
  Wherefore should love not feign him fair?
Put blood of roses in his veins,
  Weave yellow sunshines for his hair?

All ghosts of little children dead
  That wander wistful, uncaressed,
Their seeking lips by love unfed,
  She fain would cradle on her breast
For his sweet sake whose lonely head
  Has never known that tender rest.

And thus she sits, and thus she broods,
  Where drifted blossoms freak the grass;
The winds that move across her moods
  Pulse with low whispers as they pass,
And in their eerier interludes
  She hears a voice that never was.

ACROSS THE NIGHT

MUCH listening through the silences,
  Much staring through the night,
And lo! the dumb blind distances
  Are bridged with speech and sight!

Magician Thought, informed of Love,
  Hath fixed her on the air—
Oh, Love and I laughed down the fates
  And clasped her, here as there!

Across the eerie silences
  She came in headlong flight,
She stormed the serried distances,
  She trampled space and night!

Oh, foolish scientists might give
  This miracle a name—
But Love and I care but to know
  That when we called she came.

And since I find the distances
  Subservient to my thought,
And of the sentient silences
  More vital speech have wrought,

Then she and I will mock Death's self,
  For all his vaunted might—
There are no gulfs we dare not leap,
  As she leapt through the night!

SEA CHANGES

I

MORNING

We stood among the boats and nets;
  We saw the swift clouds fall,
We watched the schooners scamper in
  Before the sudden squall;—
The jolly squall strove lustily
  To whelm the sheltered street—
The merry squall that piled the seas
About the patient headland's knees
  And chased the fishing fleet.

She laughed; as if with wings her mirth
Arose and left the wingless earth
  And all tame things behind;
Rose like a bird, wild with delight
Whose briny pinions flash in flight
  Through storm and sun and wind.

Her laughter sought those skies because
  Their mood and hers were one,
For she and I were drunk with love
  And life and storm and sun!

And while she laughed, the Sun himself
  Leapt laughing through the rain
And struck his harper hand along
The ringing coast; and that wind-song
  Whose joy is mixed with pain
Forgot the undertone of grief
  And joined the jocund strain,
And over every hidden reef
Whereon the waves broke merrily
Rose jets and sprays of melody
  And leapt and laughed again.

II

MOONLIGHT

We stood among the boats and nets . .
  We marked the risen moon
Walk swaying o'er the trembling seas
  As one sways in a swoon;

The little stars, the lonely stars,
  Stole through the hollow sky,
And every sucking eddy where
The waves lapped wharf or rotten stair
Moaned like some stricken thing hid there
And strangled with its own despair
  As the shuddering tide crept by.

I loved her, and I hated her—
  Or did I hate myself because,
  Bound by obscure, strong, silken laws,
I felt myself the worshiper
  Of beauty never wholly mine?
With lures most apt to snare, entwine,
With bonds too subtle to define,
Her lighter nature mastered mine;
Herself half given, half withheld,
Her lesser spirit still compelled
Its tribute from my franker soul:
  So—rebel, slave, and worshiper!—
  I loved her and I hated her.

I gazed upon her, I, her thrall,
  And musing, murmured, "*What if death*

Were just the answer to it all?—
  Suppose some dainty dagger quaffed
  Her life in one deep eager draught?—
Suppose some amorous knife caressed
The lovely hollow of her breast?"—
She turned a mocking look to mine:
She read the thought within my eyne,
  She held me with her look—and laughed!

Now who may tell what stirs, controls,
  And shapes mad fancies into facts?
What trivial things may quicken souls
  To irrevocable, swift acts?
Now who has known, who understood,
  Wherefore some idle thing
  May stab with deadlier sting
Than well-considered insult could?—
May spur the languor of a mood
And rouse a tiger in the blood?—

Ah, Christ!—had she not laughed just when
That fancy came! . . . for then . . . and then . .
  A sudden mist dropped from the sky,

A mist swept in across the sea . . .
A mist that hid her face from me . . .
  A weeping mist all tinged with red,
A dripping mist that smelt like blood . . .
  It choked my throat, it burnt my brain . . .
And through it peered one sallow star,
  And through it rang one shriek of pain . . .
And when it passed my hands were red,
  My soul was dabbled with her blood;
And when it passed my love was dead
  And tossed upon the troubled flood.

III

MOONSET

But see! . . . the body does not sink;
  It rides upon the tide
(A starbeam on the dagger's haft),
  With staring eyes and wide . . .
And now, up from the darkling sea,
  Down from the failing moon,
Are come strange shapes to mock at me . . .
All pallid from the star-pale sea,
  White from the paling moon . . .

Or whirling fast or wheeling slow
Around, around the corpse they go,
All bloodless o'er the sickened sea
Beneath the ailing moon!

And are they only wisps of fog
That dance along the waves?
Only shapes of mist the wind
Drives along the waves?
Or are they spirits that the sea
Has cheated of their graves?
The ghosts of them that died at sea,
Of murdered men flung in the sea,
Whose bodies had no graves?—
Lost souls that haunt for evermore
The sobbing reef and hollowed shore
And always-murmuring caves?

Ah, surely something more than fog,
More than starlit mist!
For starlight never makes a sound
And fogs are ever whist—
But hearken, hearken, hearken, now,
For these sing as they dance!

As airily, as eerily,
  They wheel about and whirl,
They jeer at me, they fleer at me,
  They flout me as they swirl!
As whirling fast or swaying slow,
Reeling, wheeling, to and fro,
Around, around the corpse they go,
  They chill me with their chants!
These be neither men nor mists—
  Hearken to their chants:

Ever, ever, ever,
  Drifting like a blossom
Seaward, with the starlight
  Wan upon her bosom—
Ever when the quickened
  Heart of night is throbbing,
Ever when the trembling
  Tide sets seaward, sobbing,
Shall you see this burden
  Borne upon its ebbing:
See her drifting seaward
  Like a broken blossom,

Ever see the starlight
Kiss her bruisèd bosom.

Flight availeth nothing . . .
Still the subtle beaches
Draw you back where Horror
Walks their shingled reaches .
Ever shall your spirit
Hear the surf resounding,
Evermore the ocean
Thwarting you and bounding;
Vainly struggle inland!
Lashing you and hounding,
Still the vision hales you
From the upland reaches,
Goading you and gripping,
Binds you to the beaches!

Ever, ever, ever,
Ever shall her laughter,
Hunting you and haunting,
Mock and follow after;
Rising where the buoy-bell
Clangs across the shallows,

Leaping where the spindrift
Hurtles o'er the hollows,
Ringing where the moonlight
Gleams along the billows,
Ever, ever, ever,
Ever shall her laughter,
Hounding you and haunting,
Whip and follow after!

IV

SUNSET

I stood among the boats and nets;
The sinking sun, the angry sun,
Across the sullen wave
Laid the sudden strength of his red wrath
Like to a shaken glaive:—
Or did the sun pause in the west
To lift a sword at me,
Or was it she, or was it she,
Rose for an instant on some crest
And plucked the red blade from her breast
And brandished it at me?

THE TAVERN OF DESPAIR

THE wraiths of murdered hopes and loves
  Come whispering at the door,
Come creeping through the weeping mist
  That drapes the barren moor;
But we within have turned the key
  'Gainst Hope and Love and Care,
Where Wit keeps tryst with Folly, at
  The Tavern of Despair.

And we have come by divers ways
  To keep this merry tryst,
But few of us have kept within
  The Narrow Way, I wist;
For we are those whose ampler wits
  And hearts have proved our curse—
Foredoomed to ken the better things
  And aye to do the worse!

Long since we learned to mock ourselves;
  And from self-mockery fell

To heedless laughter in the face
  Of Heaven, Earth, and Hell.
We quiver 'neath, and mock, God's rod;
  We feel, and mock, His wrath;
We mock our own blood on the thorns
  That rim the "Primrose Path."

We mock the eerie glimmering shapes
  That range the outer wold,
We mock our own cold hearts because
  They are so dead and cold;
We flout the things we might have been
  Had self to self proved true,
We mock the roses flung away,
  We mock the garnered rue;

The fates that gibe have lessoned us;
  There sups to-night on earth
No madder crew of wastrels than
  This fellowship of mirth. . . .
(Of mirth . . . drink, fools!—nor let it flag
  Lest from the outer mist
Creep in that other company
  Unbidden to the tryst.)

We're grown so fond of paradox
  Perverseness holds us thrall,
So what each jester loves the best
  He mocks the most of all;
But as the jest and laugh go round,
  Each in his neighbor's eyes
Reads, while he flouts his heart's desire,
  The knowledge that he lies.

Not one of us but had some pearls
  And flung them to the swine,
Not one of us but had some gift—
  Some spark of fire divine—
Each might have been God's minister
  In the temple of some art—
Each feels his gift perverted move
  Wormlike through his dry heart.

If God called Azrael to Him now
  And bade Death bend the bow
Against the saddest heart that beats
  Here on this earth below,
Not any sobbing breast would gain
  The guerdon of that barb—

Whose shout aye loudest rings, and whose
  The maddest cranks and quips—
Who mints his soul to laughter's coin
  And wastes it with his lips—
Has grown too sad for sighs and seeks
  To cheat himself with mirth;
We fools self-doomed to motley are
  The weariest wights on earth!

But yet, for us whose brains and hearts
  Strove aye in paths perverse,
Doomed still to know the better things
  And still to do the worse,—
What else is there remains for us
  But make a jest of care
And set the rafters ringing, in
  Our Tavern of Despair?

COLORS AND SURFACES

A GOLDEN LAD

(D. V. M.)

> "Golden lads and lasses must
> Like chimney-sweepers come to dust."
>
> —SHAKESPEARE.

So young, but already the splendor
  Of genius robed him about—
Already the dangerous, tender
  Regard of the gods marked him out—

(On whom the burden and duty
  They bind, at his earliest breath,
Of showing their own grave beauty,
  They love and they crown with death.)

We were of one blood, but the olden
  Rapt poets spake out in his tone;
We were of one blood, but the golden
  Rathe promise was his, his alone.

And ever his great eye glistened
  With visions I could not see,
Ever he thrilled and listened
  To voices withholden from me.

Young lord of the realms of fancy,
  The bright dreams flocked to his call
Like sprites that the necromancy
  Of a Prospero holds in thrall—

Quick visions that served and attended,
  Elusive and hovering things,
With a quiver of joy in the splendid
  Wild sweep of their luminous wings;

He dwelt in an alien glamor,
  He wrought of its gleams a crown,—
But the world, with its cruelty and clamor,
  Broke him and beat him down;

So he passed; he was worn, he was weary,
  He was slain at the touch of life;—
With a smile that was wistful and eerie
  He passed from the senseless strife;—

So he ceased (is their humor satiric,
  These gods that make perfect and blight?)--
He ceased like an exquisite lyric
  That dies on the breast of night.

THE SAGE AND THE WOMAN

'TWIXT ancient Beersheba and Dan
Another such a caravan
Dazed Palestine had never seen
As that which bore Sabea's queen
Up from the fain and flaming South
To slake her yearning spirit's drouth
  At wisdom's pools, with Solomon.

With gifts of scented sandalwood,
And labdanum, and cassia-bud,
With spicy spoils of Araby
And camel-loads of ivory
And heavy cloths that glanced and shone
With inwrought pearl and beryl-stone
  She came, a bold Sabean girl.

And did she find him grave, or gay?
Perchance his palace breathed that day

With psalters sounding solemnly—
Or cymbals' merrier minstrelsy—
Perchance the wearied monarch heard
Some loose-tongued prophet's meddling word;—
  None knows, no one—but Solomon!

She looked—with eyne wherein were blent
All ardors of the Orient;
She spake—all magics of the South
Were compassed in the witch's mouth;—
He thought the scarlet lips of her
More precious than En Gedi's myrrh,
  The lips of that Sabean girl;

By many an amorous sun caressed,
From lifted brow to amber breast
She gleamed in vivid loveliness—
And lithe as any leopardess—
And verily, one blames thee not
If thine own proverbs were forgot,
  O Solomon, wise Solomon!

She danced for him, and surely she
Learnt dancing from some moonlit sea

Where elfin vapors swirled and swayed
While the wild pipes of witchcraft played
Such clutching music 'twould impel
A prophet's self to dance to hell—
  So spun the light Sabean girl.

He swore her laughter had the lilt
Of chiming waters that are spilt
In sprays of spurted melody
From founts of carven porphyry,
And in the billowy turbulence
Of her dusk hair drowned soul and sense—
  Dark tides and deep, O Solomon!

Perchance unto her day belongs
His poem called the Song of Songs,
Each little lyric interval
Timed to her pulse's rise and fall;—
Or when he cried out wearily
That all things end in vanity
  Did he mean that Sabean girl?

The bright barbaric opulence,
The sun-kist Temple, Kedar's tents,—

How many a careless caravan
'Twixt Beersheba and ruined Dan,
Within these forty centuries,
Has flung their dust to many a breeze,
  With dust that was King Solomon!

But still the lesson holds as true,
O King, as when she lessoned you:
That very wise men are not wise
Until they read in Folly's eyes
The wisdom that escapes the schools,
That bids the sage revise his rules
  By light of some Sabean girl!

6

NEWS FROM BABYLON

"Archæologists have discovered a love-letter among the ruins of Babylon."—*Newspaper report.*

The world hath just one tale to tell, and it is very old,
A little tale—a simple tale—a tale that's easy told:
"There was a youth in Babylon who greatly loved a
maid!"
The world hath just one song to sing, but sings it
unafraid,
A little song—a foolish song—the only song it hath:
"There was a youth in Ascalon who loved a girl in
Gath!"

Homer clanged it, Omar twanged it, Greece and
Persia knew!—
Nimrod's reivers, Hiram's weavers, Hindu, Kurd,
and Jew—
Crowning Tyre, Troy afire, they have dreamed
the dream;
Tiber-side and Nilus-tide brightened with the
gleam—

Oh, the suing, sighing, wooing, sad and merry
hours,
Blisses tasted, kisses wasted, building Babel's
towers!
Hearts were aching, hearts were breaking, lashes
wet with dew,
When the ships touched the lips of islands Sappho
knew;
Yearning breasts and burning breasts, cold at last,
are hid
Amid the glooms of carven tombs in Khufu's
pyramid—
Though the sages, down the ages, smile their cynic
doubt,
Man and maid, unafraid, put the schools to rout;
Seek to chain love and retain love in the bonds of
breath,
Vow to hold love, bind and fold love even unto
death!

The dust of forty centuries has buried Babylon,
And out of all her lovers dead rises only one;
Rises with a song to sing and laughter in his eyes,
The old song—the only song—for all the rest are lies!

For, oh, the world has just one dream, and it is very
old—
'Tis youth's dream—a silly dream—but it is flushed
with gold!

A RHYME OF THE ROADS

PEARL-SLASHED and purple and crimson and
    fringed with gray mist of the hills,
The pennons of morning advance to the music of
    rock-fretted rills,
The dumb forest quickens to song, and the little
    gusts shout as they fling
A floor-cloth of orchard bloom down for the flash-
    ing, quick feet of the Spring.

To the road, gipsy-heart, thou and I! 'Tis the
    mad piper, Spring, who is leading;
'Tis the pulse of his piping that throbs through
    the brain, irresistibly pleading;
Full-blossomed, deep-bosomed, fain woman, light-
    footed, lute-throated and fleet,
We have drunk of the wine of this Wanderer's song;
    let us follow his feet!

Like raveled red girdles flung down by some
hoidenish goddess in mirth
The tangled roads reach from rim unto utter-
most rim of the earth—
We will weave of these strands a strong net, we
will snare the bright wings of delight,—
We will make of these strings a sweet lute that
will shame the low wind-harps of night.

The clamor of tongues and the clangor of trades
in the peevish packed street,
The arrogant, jangling Nothings, with iterant, dis-
sonant beat,
The clattering, senseless endeavor with dross of
mere gold for its goal,
These have sickened the senses and wearied the
brain and straitened the soul.

"Come forth and be cleansed of the folly of strife
for things worthless of strife,
Come forth and gain life and grasp God by fore-
going gains worthless of life"—

It was thus spake the wizard wildwood, low-
voiced to the hearkening heart,
It was thus sang the jovial hills, and the harper
sun bore part.

O woman, whose blood as my blood with the fire
of the Spring is aflame,
We did well, when the red roads called, that we
heeded the call and came—
Came forth to the sweet wise silence where soul
may speak sooth unto soul,
Vine-wreathed and vagabond Love, with the goal
of Nowhere for our goal!

What planet-crowned Dusk that wanders the
steeps of our firmament there
Hath gems that may match with the dew-opals
meshed in thine opulent hair?
What wind-witch that skims the curled billows
with feet they are fain to caress
Hath sandals so wing'd as thine art with a god-
like carelessness?

And dare we not dream this is heaven?—to wander thus on, ever on,
Through the hush-heavy valleys of space, up the flushing red slopes of the dawn?—
For none that seeks rest shall find rest till he ceaseth his striving for rest,
And the gain of the quest is the joy of the road that allures to the quest.

THE LAND OF YESTERDAY

AND I would seek the country town
Amid green meadows nestled down
If I could only find the way
Back to the Land of Yesterday!

How I would thrust the miles aside,
  Rush up the quiet lane, and then,
Just where her roses laughed in pride,
  Find her among the flowers again.
I'd slip in silently and wait
Until she saw me by the gate,
And then . . . read through a blur of tears
Quick pardon for the selfish years.

This time, this time, I would not wait
For that brief wire that said, *Too late!*—
If I could only find the way
Into the Land of Yesterday.

I wonder if her roses yet
  Lift up their heads and laugh with pride,
And if her phlox and mignonette
  Have heart to blossom by their side;
I wonder if the dear old lane
Still chirps with robins after rain,
And if the birds and banded bees
Still rob her early cherry-trees. . . .

I wonder, if I went there now,
How everything would seem, and how—
But no! not now; there is no way
Back to the Land of Yesterday.

OCTOBER

CEASE to call him sad and sober,
Merriest of months, October!
Patron of the bursting bins,
Reveler in wayside inns,
I can nowhere find a trace
Of the pensive in his face;
There is mingled wit and folly,
But the madcap lacks the grace
Of a thoughtful melancholy.
Spendthrift of the seasons' gold,
How he flings and scatters out
Treasure filched from summer-time!—
Never ruffling squire of old
Better loved a tavern bout
When Prince Hal was in his prime.
Doublet slashed with gold and green;
Cloak of crimson; changeful sheen,
Of the dews that gem his breast;
Frosty lace about his throat;

Scarlet plumes that flaunt and float
Backward in a gay unrest—
Where's another gallant drest
With such tricksy gaiety,
Such unlessoned vanity?
With his amber afternoons
And his pendant poets' moons—
With his twilights dashed with rose
From the red-lipped afterglows—
With his vocal airs at dawn
Breathing hints of Helicon—
Bacchanalian bees that sip
Where his cider-presses drip—
With the winding of the horn
Where his huntsmen meet the morn—
With his every piping breeze
Shaking from familiar trees
Apples of Hesperides—
With the chuckle, chirp, and trill
Of his jolly brooks that spill
Mirth in tangled madrigals
Down pebble-dappled waterfalls—
(Brooks that laugh and make escape
Through wild arbors where the grape

Purples with a promise of
Racy vintage rare as love)—
With his merry, wanton air,
Mirth and vanity and folly
Why should he be made to bear
Burden of some melancholy
Song that swoons and sinks with care?
Cease to call him sad or sober,—
He's a jolly dog, October!

CHANT OF THE CHANGING HOURS

THE Hours passed by, a fleet, confusèd crowd;
With wafture of blown garments bright as fire,
Light, light of foot and laughing, morning-browed,
And where they trod the jonquil and the briar
Thrilled into jocund life, the dreaming dells
Waked to a morrice chime of jostled bells;—
They danced! they danced! to piping such as flings
The garnered music of a million Springs
Into one single, keener ecstasy;—
One paused and shouted to my questionings:
"Lo, I am Youth; I bid thee follow me!"

The Hours passed by; they paced, great lords and proud,
Crowned on with sunlight, robed in rich attire;
Before their conquering word the brute deed bowed,
And Ariel fancies served their large desire;

They spake, and roused the musèd soul that dwells
In dust, or, smiling, shaped new heavens and
hells,
Dethroned old gods and made blind beggars kings:
"And what art thou," I cried to one, "that brings
His mistress, for a brooch, the Galaxy?"—
"I am the plumèd Thought that soars and sings:
Lo, I am Song; I bid thee follow me!"

The Hours passed by, with veilèd eyes endowed
Of dream, and parted lips that scarce suspire,
To breathing dusk and arrowy moonlight vowed,
South wind and shadowy grove and murmuring
lyre;—
Swaying they moved, as drows'd of wizard spells
Or tranc'd with sight of recent miracles,
And yet they trembled, down their folded wings
Quivered the hint of sweet withholden things,
Ah, bitter-sweet in their intensity!
One paused and said unto my wonderings:
"Lo, I am Love; I bid thee follow me!"

The Hours passed by, through huddled cities loud
With witless hate and stale with stinking mire:

So cowlèd monks might march with bier and shroud
Down streets plague-spotted toward some cleansing pyre;—
Yet, lo! strange lilies bloomed in lightless cells,
And passionate spirits burst their clayey shells
And sang the stricken hope that bleeds and clings:
Earth's bruisèd heart beat in the throbbing strings,
And joy still struggled through the threnody!
One stern Hour said unto my marvelings:
"Lo, I am Life; I bid thee follow me!"

The Hours passed by, the stumbling hours and cowed,
Uncertain, prone to tears and childish ire,—
The wavering hours that drift like any cloud
At whim of winds or fortunate or dire,—
The feeble shapes that any chance expells;
Their wisdom useless, lacking the blood that swells
The tensèd vein: the hot, swift tide that stings
With life. Ah, wise! but naked to the slings
Of fate, and plagued of youthful memory!
A cracked voice broke upon my pityings:
"Lo, I am Age; I bid thee follow me!"

Ah, Youth! we dallied by the babbling wells
Where April all her lyric secret tells;—
Ah, Song! we sped our bold imaginings
As far as yon red planet's triple rings;—
O Life! O Love! I followed, followed thee!
There waits one word to end my journeyings:
"Lo, I am Death; I bid thee follow me!"

7

DREAMS AND DUST

SELVES

My dust in ruined Babylon
Is blown along the level plain,
And songs of mine at dawn have soared
Above the blue Sicilian main.

We are ourselves, and not ourselves . . .
For ever thwarting pride and will
Some forebear's passion leaps from death
To claim a vital license still.

Ancestral lusts that slew and died,
Resurgent, swell each living vein;
Old doubts and faiths, new panoplied,
Dispute the mastery of the brain.

The love of liberty that flames
From written rune and stricken reed
Shook the hot hearts of swordsmen sires
At Marathon and Runnymede.

What are these things we call our "selves"? . . .
Have I not shouted, sobbed, and died
In the bright surf of spears that broke
Where Greece rolled back the Persian tide?

Are we who breathe more quick than they
Whose bones are dust within the tomb?
Nay, as I write, what gray old ghosts
Murmur and mock me from the gloom. . . .

They call . . . across strange seas they call,
Strange seas, and haunted coasts of time. . . .
They startle me with wordless songs
To which the Sphinx hath known the rhyme.

Our hearts swell big with dead men's hates,
Our eyes sting hot with dead men's tears;
We are ourselves, but not ourselves,
Born heirs, but serfs, to all the years!

I rode with Nimrod . . . strove at Troy . . .
A slave I stood in crowning Tyre,
A queen looked on me and I loved
And died to compass my desire.

THE WAGES

EARTH loves to gibber o'er her dross,
  Her golden souls, to waste;
The cup she fills for her god-men
  Is a bitter cup to taste.

Who sees the gyves that bind mankind
  And strives to strike them off
Shall gain the hissing hate of fools,
  Thorns, and the ingrate's scoff.

Who storms the moss-grown walls of eld
  And beats some falsehood down
Shall pass the pallid gates of death
  Sans laurel, love or crown;

For him who fain would teach the world
  The world holds hate in fee—
For Socrates, the hemlock cup;
  For Christ, Gethsemane.

IN MARS, WHAT AVATAR?

"In Vishnu-land, what avatar?"
—BROWNING.

PERCHANCE the dying gods of Earth
Are destined to another birth,
And worn-out creeds regain their worth
  In the kindly air of other stars—
What lords of life and light hold sway
In the myriad worlds of the Milky Way?
  What avatars in Mars?

What Aphrodites from the seas
That lap the plunging Pleiades
  Arise to spread afar
The dream that was the soul of Greece?
  In Mars, what avatar?

Which hundred moons are wan with love
  For dull Endymions?
Which hundred moons hang tranced above
  Audacious Ajalons?

What Holy Grail lures errants pale
  Through the wastes of yonder star?
What fables sway the Milky Way?
  In Mars, what avatar?

When morning skims with crimson wings
  Across the meres of Mercury,
What dreaming Memnon wakes and sings
  Of miracles on Mercury?
What Christs, what avatars,
Claim Mars?

THE GOD-MAKER, MAN

Nevermore
  Shall the shepherds of Arcady follow
Pan's moods as he lolls by the shore
  Of the mere, or lies hid in the hollow;
Nevermore
  Shall they start at the sound of his reed-fashioned
    flute;

Fallen mute
  Are the strings of Apollo,
His lyre and his lute;
  And the lips of the Memnons are mute
Evermore;
  And the gods of the North,—are they dead or
    forgetful,
Our Odin and Baldur and Thor?
  Are they drunk, or grown weary of worship and
    fretful,
Our Odin and Baldur and Thor?

And into what night have the Orient deities
strayed?
Swart gods of the Nile, in dusk splendors arrayed,
Brooding Isis and somber Osiris,
You were gone ere the fragile papyrus,
(That bragged you eternal!) decayed.

The avatars
But illumine their limited evens
And vanish like plunging stars;
They are fixed in the whirling heavens
No firmer than falling stars;
Brief lords of the changing soul, they pass
Like a breath from the face of a glass,
Or a blossom of summer blown shallop-like over
The clover
And tossed tides of grass.

Sink to silence the psalms and the pæans
The shibboleths shift, and the faiths,
And the temples that challenged the æons
Are tenanted only by wraiths;
Swoon to silence the cymbals and psalters,
The worships grow senseless and strange,

Yes, nothing seems changeless, but Change.
And yet, through the creed-wrecking years,
One story for ever appears;
The tale of a City Supernal—
The whisper of Something eternal—
A passion, a hope, and a vision
  That peoples the silence with Powers;
A fable of meadows Elysian
  Where Time enters not with his Hours;—
Manifold are the tale's variations,
  Race and clime ever tinting the dreams,
Yet its essence, through endless mutations,
  Immutable gleams.

Deathless, though godheads be dying,
  Surviving the creeds that expire,
Illogical, reason-defying,
  Lives that passionate, primal desire;
Insistent, persistent, forever
Man cries to the silences, "*Never*

Shall Death reign the lord of the soul,
Shall the dust be the ultimate goal—
I will storm the black bastions of Night!
I will tread where my vision has trod,
I will set in the darkness a light,
In the vastness, a god!"

As the forehead of Man grows broader, so do his creeds;
And his gods they are shaped in his image, and mirror his needs;
And he clothes them with thunders and beauty, he clothes them with music and fire;
Seeing not, as he bows by their altars, that he worships his own desire;
And mixed with his trust there is terror, and mixed with his madness is ruth,
And every man grovels in error, yet every man glimpses a truth.

For all of the creeds are false, and all of the creeds are true;
And low at the shrines where my brothers bow, there will I bow, too;

For no form of a god, and no fashion
Man has made in his desperate passion
But is worthy some worship of mine;—
Not too hot with a gross belief,
  Nor yet too cold with pride,
I will bow me down where my brothers bow,
  Humble—but open-eyed!

UNREST

A FIERCE unrest seethes at the core
  Of all existing things:
It was the eager wish to soar
  That gave the gods their wings.

From what flat wastes of cosmic slime,
  And stung by what quick fire,
Sunward the restless races climb!—
  Men risen out of mire!

There throbs through all the worlds that are
  This heart-beat hot and strong,
And shaken systems, star by star,
  Awake and glow in song.

But for the urge of this unrest
  These joyous spheres were mute;
But for the rebel in his breast
  Had man remained a brute.

When baffled lips demanded speech,
  Speech trembled into birth—
(One day the lyric word shall reach
  From earth to laughing earth)—

When man's dim eyes demanded light
  The light he sought was born—
His wish, a Titan, scaled the height
  And flung him back the morn!

From deed to dream, from dream to deed,
  From daring hope to hope,
The restless wish, the instant need,
  Still lashed him up the slope!

. . . .

I sing no governed firmament,
  Cold, ordered, regular—
I sing the stinging discontent
  That leaps from star to star!

THE PILTDOWN SKULL

WHAT was his life, back yonder
  In the dusk where time began,
This beast uncouth with the jaw of an ape
  And the eye and brain of a man?—
Work, and the wooing of woman,
  Fight, and the lust of fight,
Play, and the blind beginnings
  Of an Art that groped for light?—

In the wonder of redder mornings,
  By the beauty of brighter seas,
Did he stand, the world's first thinker,
  Scorning his clan's decrees?—
Seeking, with baffled eyes,
In the dumb, inscrutable skies,
A name for the greater glory
  That only the dreamer sees?

One day, when the afterglows,
  Like quick and sentient things,

With a rush of their vast, wild wings,
Rose out of the shaken ocean
As great birds rise from the sod,
Did the shock of their sudden splendor
Stir him and startle and thrill him,
Grip him and shake him and fill him
With a sense as of heights untrod?—
Did he tremble with hope and vision,
And grasp at a hint of God?

London stands where the mammoth
Caked shag flanks with slime—
And what are our lives that inherit
The treasures of all time?
Work, and the wooing of woman,
Fight, and the lust of fight,
A little play (and too much toil!)
With an Art that gropes for light;
And now and then a dreamer,
Rapt, from his lonely sod
Looks up and is thrilled and startled
With a fleeting sense of God!

THE SEEKER

The creeds he wrought of dream and thought
  Fall from him at the touch of life,
  His old gods fail him in the strife—
Withdrawn, the heavens he sought!

Vanished, the miracles that led,
  The cloud at noon, the flame at night;
The vision that he wing'd and sped
  Falls backward, baffled, from the height;

Yet in the wreck of these he stands
  Upheld by something grim and strong;
  Some stubborn instinct lifts a song
And nerves him, heart and hands:

He does not dare to call it hope;—
  It is not aught that seeks reward—

It touches something elder far
  Than faith or creed or thought in man,
  It was ere yet these lived and ran
Like light from star to star;

It touches that stark, primal need
  That from unpeopled voids and vast
Fashioned the first crude, childish creed,—
  And still shall fashion, till the last!

For one word is the tale of men:
  They fling their icons to the sod,
  And having trampled down a god
They seek a god again!

Stripped of his creeds inherited,
  Bereft of all his sires held true,
Amid the wreck of visions dead
  He thrills at touch of visions new. . . .

He wings another Dream for flight. . . .
  He seeks beyond the outmost dawn
  A god he set there . . . and, anon,
Drags that god from the height!

. . . . . .

But aye from ruined faiths and old
  That droop and die, fall bruisèd seeds;
And when new flowers and faiths unfold
  They're lovelier flowers, they're kindlier creeds.

THE AWAKENING

THE steam, the reek, the fume, of prayer
  Blown outward for a million years,
  Becomes a mist between the spheres,
And waking Sentience struggles there.

Prayer still creates the boon we pray;
  And gods we've hoped for, from those hopes
Will gain sufficient form one day
  And in full godhood storm the slopes
Where ancient Chaos, stark and gray,
Already trembles for his sway.

When that the restless worlds would fly
  Their wish created rapid wings,
But not till æons had passed by
  With dower of many idler things;
And when dumb flesh demanded speech
  Speech struggled to the lips at last;—
  Now the unpeopled Void, and vast,

Clean to that uttermost blank beach
Whereto the boldest thought may reach
  That voyages from the vaguest past—
  (Dim realm and ultimate of space)—
Is vexed and troubled, stirs and shakes,
In prescience of a god that wakes,
  Born of man's wish to see God's face!

The endless, groping, dumb desires,—
  The climbing incense thick and sweet,
The lovely purpose that aspires,
  The wraiths of vapor wing'd and fleet
  That rise and run with eager feet
Forth from a myriad altar fires:
  All these become a mist that fills
The vales and chasms nebular;
  A shaping Soul that moves and thrills
The wastes between red star and star!

A SONG OF MEN

OUT of the soil and the slime,
Reeking, they climb,

Out of the muck and the mire,
Rank, they aspire;

Filthy with murder and mud,
Black with shed blood,

Lust and passion and clay—
Dying, they slay;

Stirred by vague hints of a goal,
Seeking a soul!

Groping through terror and night
Up to the light:

Life in the dust and the clod
Sensing a God;

Flushed of the glamor and gleam
Caught from a dream;

Stained of the struggle and toil,
Stained of the soil,

Ally of God in the end—
Helper and friend—

Hero and prophet and priest
Out of the beast!

THE NOBLER LESSON

Christ was of virgin birth, and, being slain,
The creedists say, He rose from death again.
Oh, futile age-long talk of death and birth!—
His life, that is the one thing wonder-worth;
Not how He came, but how He lived on earth.
For if gods stoop, and with quaint jugglery
Mock nature's laws, how shall that profit thee?—
The nobler lesson is that mortals can
Grow godlike through this baffled front of man!

AT LAST

EACH race has died and lived and fought for the
"true" gods of that poor race,
Unconsciously, divinest thought of each race gilding its god's face.
And every race that lives and dies shall make itself
some other gods,
Shall build, with mingled truth and lies, new icons
from the world-old clods.
Through all the tangled creeds and dreams and
shifting shibboleths men hold
The false-and-true, inwoven, gleams: a matted
mass of dross and gold.
Prove, then, thy gods in thine own soul; all others'
gods, for thee, are vain;
Nor swerved be, struggling for the goal, by bribe
of joy nor threat of pain.

As skulls grow broader, so do faiths; as old tongues
die, old gods die, too,

And only ghosts of gods and wraiths may meet
the backward-gazer's view.
Where, where the faiths of yesterday? Ah,
whither vanished, whither gone?
Say, what Apollos drive to-day adown the flaming
slopes of dawn?
Oh, does the blank past hide from view forgotten
Christs, to be reborn,
The future tremble where some new Messiah-
Memnon sings the morn?
Of all the worlds, say any earth, like dust wind-
harried to and fro,
Shall give the next Prometheus birth; but say—
at last—you do not know.

How should I know what dawn may gleam beyond
the gates of darkness there?—
Which god of all the gods men dream? Why
should I whip myself to care?
Whichever over all hath place hath shaped and
made me what I am;
Hath made me strong to front his face, to dare
to question though he damn.

Perhaps to cringe and cower and bring a shrine
a forced and faithless faith
Is far more futile than to fling your laughter in
the face of Death.
For writhe or whirl in dervish rout, they are not
flattered there on high,
Or sham belief to hide a doubt—no gods are mine
that love a lie!
Nor gods that beg belief on earth with portents
that some seer foretells—
Is life itself not wonder-worth that we must cry
for miracles?
Is it not strange enough we breathe? Does every-
thing not God reveal?
Or must we ever weave and wreathe some creed
that shall his face conceal?
Some creed of which its prophets cry it holds
the secret's all-in-all:
Some creed which ever bye and bye doth crumble,
totter, to its fall!
Say any dream of all the dreams that drift and
darkle, glint and glow,
Holds most of truth within its gleams; but say
—at last—you do not know.

Oh, say the soul, from star to star, with victory
wing'd, leap on through space
And scale the bastioned nights that bar the secret's
inner dwelling-place;
Or say it ever roam dim glades where pallid
wraiths of long-dead moons
Flit like blown feathers through the shades, borne
on the breath of sobbing tunes:
Say any tide of any time, of all the tides that ebb
and flow,
Shall buoy us on toward any clime; but say—at
last—you do not know!

LYRICS

"KING PANDION, HE IS DEAD"

"King Pandion, he is dead;
All thy friends are lapp'd in lead."
—SHAKESPEARE.

DREAMERS, drinkers, rebel youth,
Where's the folly free and fine
You and I mistook for truth?
Wits and wastrels, friends of wine,
Wags and poets, friends of mine,
Gleams and glamors all are fled,
Fires and frenzies half divine!
King Pandion, he is dead!

Time's unmannerly, uncouth!
Here's the crow's-foot for a sign!
And, upon our brows, forsooth,
Wits and wastrels, friends of wine,
Time hath set his mark malign;
Frost has touched us, heart and head,
Cooled the blood and dulled the eyne:
King Pandion, he is dead!

Time's a tyrant without ruth:—
  Fancies used to bloom and twine
Round a common tavern booth,
  Wits and wastrels, friends of wine,
  In that youth of mine and thine!
'Tis for youth the feast is spread;
  When we dine now—we but dine!—
King Pandion, he is dead!

How our dreams would glow and shine,
Wits and wastrels, friends of wine,
Ere the drab Hour came that said:
King Pandion, he is dead!

DAVID TO BATHSHEBA

Very red are the roses of Sharon,
But redder thy mouth,
There is nard, there is myrrh, in En Gedi,
From the uplands of Lebanon, heavy
With balsam, the winds
Drift freighted and scented and cedarn—
But thy mouth is more precious than spices!

Thy breasts are twin lilies of Kedron;
White lilies, that sleep
In the shallows where loitering Kedron
Broadens out and is lost in the Jordan;
Globèd lilies, so white
That David, thy King, thy belovèd
Declareth them meet for his gardens.

Under the stars very strangely
The still waters gleam;
Deep down in the waters of Hebron

The soul of the starlight is sunken,
But deep in thine eyes
Stirs a more wonderful secret
Than pools ever learn of the starlight.

THE JESTERS

A TOAST to the Fools!
  Pierrot, Pantaloon,
Harlequin, Clown,
  Merry-Andrew, Buffoon—
Touchstone and Triboulet—all of the tribe.—
Dancer and jester and singer and scribe.
We sigh over Yorick—(unfortunate fool,
Ten thousand Hamlets have fumbled *his* skull!)—
But where is the Hamlet to weep o'er the biers
  Of his brothers?
And where is the poet solicits our tears
  For the others?
They have passed from the world and left never
    a sign,
  And few of us now have the courage to sing
  That their whimsies made life a more livable
    thing—
We, that are left of the line,
Let us drink to the jesters—in gooseberry wine!

Then here's to the Fools!
Flouting the sages
Through history's pages
And driving the dreary old seers into rages—
The humbugging Magis
Who prate that the wages
Of Folly are Death—toast the Fools of all ages!
They have ridden like froth down the whirlpools
        of time,
  They have jingled their caps in the councils of
        state,
They have snared half the wisdom of life in a
        rhyme,
  And tripped into nothingness grinning at fate—
Ho, brothers mine,
Brim up the glasses with gooseberry wine!

Though the prince with his firman,
The judge in his ermine,
Affirm and determine
  Bold words need the whip,
Let them spare us the rod and remit us the
        sermon,
  For Death has a quip

Of the tomb and the vermin
  That will silence at last the most impudent lip!
Is the world but a bubble, a bauble, a joke?
Heigho, Brother Fools, now your bubble is broke,
Do you ask for a tear?—or is it worth while?
Here's a sigh for you, then—but it ends in a smile!
Ho, Brother Death,
We would laugh at you, too—if you spared us the
        breath!

"MARY, MARY, QUITE CONTRARY"

"Mary, Mary, quite contrary,
  How does your garden grow?
 With silver bells and cockle-shells
  And pretty maids all in a row!"

—*Mother Goose.*

MARY, Mistress Mary,
  How does your garden grow?
From your uplands airy,
Mary, Mistress Mary,
Float the chimes of faery
  When the breezes blow!
Mary, Mistress Mary,
  How does your garden grow?

With flower-maidens, singing
  Among the morning hills—
With silvern bells a-ringing,
With flower-maidens singing,
With vocal lilies, springing
  By chanting daffodils;
With flower-maidens, singing
  Among the morning hills!

THE TRIOLET

YOUR triolet should glimmer
  Like a butterfly;
In golden light, or dimmer,
Your triolet should glimmer,
Tremble, turn, and shimmer,
  Flash, and flutter by;
Your triolet should glimmer
  Like a butterfly.

FROM THE BRIDGE

HELD and thrilled by the vision
 I stood, as the twilight died,
Where the great bridge soars like a song
 Over the crawling tide—

Stood on the middle arch—
 And night flooded in from the bay,
And wonderful under the stars
 Before me the city lay;

Girdled with swinging waters—
 Guarded by ship on ship—
A gem that the strong old ocean
 Held in his giant grip;

There was play of shadows above
 And drifting gleams below,
And magic of shifting waves
 That darkle and glance and glow;

Dusky and purple and splendid,
  Banded with loops of light,
The tall towers rose like pillars,
  Lifting the dome of night;

The gliding cars of traffic
  Slid swiftly up and down
Like monsters, fiery mailed,
  Leaping across the town.

Not planned with a thought of beauty;
  Built by a lawless breed;
Builded of lust for power,
  Builded of gold and greed.

Risen out of the trader's
  Brutal and sordid wars—
And yet, behold! a city
  Wonderful under the stars!

"PALADINS, PALADINS, YOUTH NOBLE-HEARTED"

GALAHADS, Galahads, Percivals, gallop!
Bayards, to the saddle!—the clangorous trumpets,
Hoarse with their ecstasy, call to the mellay.
Paladins, Paladins, Rolands flame-hearted,
Olivers, Olivers, follow the bugles!

Girt with the glory and glamor of power,
Error sits throned in the high place of justice;
Paladins, Paladins, youth noble-hearted,
Saddle and spear, for the battle-flags beckon!
Thrust the keen steel through the throat of the liar.

Star (or San Grael) that illumines thy pathway,
Follow it, follow that far Ideal!—
Thine not the guerdon to gain it or grasp it;
Soul of thee, passing, ascendeth unto it,
Augmenting its brightness for them that come
after.

Heed then the call of the trumpets, the trumpets,
Hoarse with the fervor, the frenzy of battle,—
Paladins, Paladins, saddle! to saddle!
Bide not, abide not, God's bugles are calling!—
Thrust the sharp sword through the heart of the
liar.

"MY LANDS, NOT THINE"

My lands, not thine, we look upon,
Friend Crœsus, hill and vale and lawn.
  Mine every woodland madrigal,
  And mine thy singing waterfall
That vaguely hints of Helicon.

Mark how thine upland slopes have drawn
A golden glory from the dawn!—
Fool's gold?—thy dullness proves them all
    My lands—not thine!

For when all title-deeds are gone,
Still, still will satyr, nymph, and faun
  Through brake and covert pipe and call
  In dances bold and bacchanal—
For them, for me, you hold in pawn,
    My lands—not thine!

TO A DANCING DOLL

FORMAL, quaint, precise, and trim,
  You begin your steps demurely—
There's a spirit almost prim
  In the feet that move so surely,
So discreetly, to the chime
Of the music that so sweetly
                    Marks the time.

But the chords begin to tinkle
                    Quicker,
And your feet they flash and flicker—
                    Twinkle!—
Flash and flutter to a tricksy
                    Fickle meter;
And you foot it like a pixie—
                    Only fleeter!

Not our current, dowdy
                    Things—

"Turkey-trots" and rowdy
Flings—
For they made you overseas
In politer times than these,
In an age when grace could please,
Ere St. Vitus
Clutched and shook us, spine and knees,—
Loosed a plague of jerks to smite us!

Well, our day is far more brisk
And our manner rather slacker),
And you are nothing more than bisque
And lacquer—
But you shame us with the graces
Of courtlier times and places
When the cheap
And vulgar wasn't "art"—
When the faunal prance and leap
Weren't "smart."

Have we lost the trick of wedding
Grace to pleasure?
Must we clown it at the bidding
Of some tawdry, common measure?

Can't you school us in the graces
Of your pose and dainty paces?—
Now the chords begin to tinkle
Quicker—
And your feet they flash and flicker—
Twinkle!—
And you mock us as you featly
Swing and flutter to the chime
Of the music-box that sweetly
Marks the time!

LOWER NEW YORK—A STORM

White wing'd below the darkling clouds
  The driven sea-gulls wheel;
The roused sea flings a storm against
  The towers of stone and steel.

The very voice of ocean rings
  Along the shaken street—
Dusk, storm, and beauty whelm the world
  Where sea and city meet—

But what care they for flashing wings,
  Quick beauty, loud refrain,
These huddled thousands, deaf and blind
  To all but greed and gain?

AT SUNSET

The sun-god stooped from out the sky
  To kiss the flushing sea,
While all the winds of all the world
  Made jovial melody;
The night came hurrying up to hide
  The lovers with her tent;
The governed thunders, rank on rank,
  Stood mute with wonderment;
The pale worn moon, a jealous shade,
  Peered from the firmament;
The early stars, the curious stars,
  Came peering forth to see
What mighty nuptials shook the world
  With such an ecstasy
Whenas the sun-god left the sky
  To mingle with the sea.

A CHRISTMAS GIFT

ALACK-A-DAY for poverty!
What jewels my mind doth give to thee!

Carved agate stone porphyrogene,
Green emerald and beryl green,
Deep sapphine and pale amethyst,
Sly opal, cloaking with a mist
The levin of its love elate,
Shy brides' pearls, flushed and delicate,
Sea-colored lapis lazuli,
Sardonyx and chalcedony,
Enkindling diamond, candid gold,
Red rubies and red garnets bold:
And all their humors should be blent
  In one intolerable blaze,
Barbaric, fierce, and opulent,
  To dazzle him that dared to gaze!

Alack-a-day for poverty:
My rhymes are all you get of me!
Yet, if your heart receive, behold!
The worthless words are set in gold.

SILVIA

I STILL remember how she moved
Among the rathe, wild blooms she loved,
(When Spring came tip-toe down the slopes,
Atremble 'twixt her doubts and hopes,
Half fearful and all virginal)—
How Silvia sought this dell to call
Her flowers into full festival,
And chid them with this madrigal:

"*The busy spider hangs the brush*
  With filmy gossamers,
The frogs are croaking in the creek,
  The sluggish blacksnake stirs,
But still the ground is bare of bloom
  Beneath the fragrant firs.

"*Arise, arise, O briar rose,*
  And sleepy violet!
Awake, awake, anemone,
  Your wintry dreams forget—

For shame, you tardy marigold,
Are you not budded yet?

"*The Swallow's back, and claims the eaves*
That last year were his home;
The Robin follows where the plow
Breaks up the crusted loam;
And Red-wings spies the Thrush and pipes:
'Look! Speckle-breast is come!'

"*Up, blooms! and storm the wooded slopes,*
The lowlands and the plain—
Blow, jonquil, blow your golden horn
Across the ranks of rain!
To arms! to arms! and put to flight
The Winter's broken train!"

She paused beside this selfsame rill,
And as she ceased, a daffodil
Held up reproachfully his head
And fluttered into speech, and said:

"*Chide not the flowers! You little know*
Of all their travail 'neath the snow,

Their struggling hours
Of choking sorrow underground.
Chide not the flowers!
You little guess of that profound
And blind, dumb agony of ours!
Yet, victor here beside the rill,
I greet the light that I have found,
A Daffodil!"

And when the Daffodil was done
A boastful Marigold spake on:

"*Oh, chide the white frost, if you choose,*
The heavy clod, so hard to loose,
The preying powers
Of worm and insect underground.
Chide not the flowers!
For spite of scathe and cruel wound,
Unconquered by the sunless hours,
I rise in regal pride, a bold
And golden-hearted, golden-crowned
Marsh Marigold!"

And when she came no more, her creek
Would not believe, but bade us seek

Hither, yon, and to and fro—
Everywhere that children go
  When the Spring
  Is on the wing
And the winds of April blow—
"I will never think her dead;
"She will come again!" it said;
And then the birds that use the vale,
Broken-hearted, turned the tale
Into syllables of song
And chirped it half a summer long:

"*Silvia, Silvia,*
  Be our Song once more,
Our vale revisit, Silvia,
  And be our Song once more:
For joy lies sleeping in the lute;
The merry pipe, the woodland flute,
And all the pleading reeds are mute
  That breathed to thee of yore.

"*Silvia, Silvia,*
  Be our Moon again,

Shine on our valley, Silvia,
And be our Moon again:
The fluffy owl and nightingale
Flit silent through the darkling vale,
Or utter only words of wail
From throats all harsh with pain.

"Silvia, Silvia,
Be Springtime, as of old;
Come clad in laughter, Silvia,
Our Springtime, as of old:
The waiting lowlands and the hills
Are tremulous with daffodils
Unblown, until thy footstep thrills
Their promise into gold."

And, musing on her here, I too
Must wonder if it can be true
She died, as other mortals do.
The thought would fit her more, to feign
That, full of life and unaware
That earth holds aught of grief or stain,
The fairies stole and hold her where
Death enters not, nor strife nor pain;—

That, drowsing on some bed of pansies,
By Titania's necromancies
Her senses were to slumber lulled,
Deeply sunken, steeped and dulled,
  And by wafture of swift pinions
She was borne out through earth's portals
  To the fairy queen's dominions,
To some land of the immortals.

THE EXPLORERS

AND some still cry: "*What is the use?*
The service rendered? What the gain?.
Heroic, yes!—but in what cause?
Have they made less one earth-borne pain?
Broadened the bounded spirit's scope?
Or died to make the dull world hope?"

Must man still be the slave of Use?—
But these men, careless and elate,
Join battle with a burly world
Or come to wrestling grips with fate,
And not for any good nor gain
Nor any fame that may befall—
But, thrilling in the clutch of life,
Heed the loud challenge and the call;—
And grown to symbols at the last,
Stand in heroic silhouette
Against horizons ultimate,
As towers that front lost seas are set;—

The reckless gesture, the strong pose,
  Sharp battle-cry flung back to Earth,
And buoyant humor, as a god
Might say: "*Lo, here my feet have trod!*"—
  There lies the meaning and the worth!

They bring no golden treasure home,
  They win no acres for their clan,
Nor dream nor deed of theirs shall mend
  The ills of man's bedeviled span—
Nor are they skilled in sleights of speech,
  (Nor overeager) to make plain
The use they serve, transcending use,—
  The gain beyond apparent gain!

EARLY AUTUMN

WITH half-hearted levies of frost that make foray,
retire, and refrain—
Ambiguous bugles that blow and that falter to
silence again—

With banners of mist that still waver above them,
advance and retreat,
The hosts of the Autumn still hide in the hills,
for a doubt stays their feet;—

But anon, with a barbaric splendor to dazzle the
eyes that behold,
And regal in raiment of purple and umber and
amber and gold,

And girt with the glamor of conquest and scarved
with red symbols of pride,
From the hills in their might and their mirth on
the steeds of the wind will they ride,

To make sport and make spoil of the Summer,
who dwells in a dream on the plain,
Still tented in opulent ease in the camps of her
indolent train.

"TIME STEALS FROM LOVE"

TIME steals from Love all but Love's wings;
And how should aught but evil things,
  Or any good but death, befall
  Him that is thrall unto Time's thrall,
Slave to the lesser of these Kings?

O heart of youth that wakes and sings!
O golden vows and golden rings!
  Life mocks you with the tale of all
    Time steals from Love!

O riven lute and writhen strings,
Dead bough whereto no blossom clings,
  The glory was ephemeral!
  Nor may our Autumn grief recall
The passion of the perished Springs
    Time steals from Love!

THE RONDEAU

Your rondeau's tale must still be light—
No bugle-call to life's stern fight!
  Rather a smiling interlude
  Memorial to some transient mood
Of idle love and gala-night.

Its manner is the merest sleight
O' hand; yet therein dwells its might,
  For if the heavier touch intrude
    Your rondeau's stale.

Fragrant and fragile, fleet and bright,
And wing'd with whim, it gleams in flight
  Like April blossoms wind-pursued
  Down aisles of tangled underwood;—
Nor be too serious when you write
    Your rondeau's tail!

VISITORS

THEY haunt me, they tease me with hinted
Withheld revelations,
The songs that I may not utter;
They lead me, they flatter, they woo me.
I follow, I follow, I snatch
At the veils of their secrets in vain—
For lo! they have left me and vanished,
The songs that I cannot sing.

There are visions elusive that come
With a quiver and shimmer of wings;—
Shapes shadows and shapes, and the murmur
Of voices;—
Shapes, that out of the twilight
Leap, and with gesture appealing
Seem to deliver a message,
And are gone 'twixt a breath and a breath;—
Shapes that race in with the waves
Moving silverly under the moon,

And are gone ere they break into foam on the rocks
And recede;—
Breathings of love from invisible
Flutes,
Blown somewhere out in the tender
Dusk,
That die on the bosom of Silence;—
Formless,
And fleeter than thought,
Vaguer than thought or emotion,
What are these visitors?

Out of the vast and uncharted
Realms that encircle the visible world,
With a glimmer of light on their pinions,
They rush . . .
They waver, they vanish,
Leaving me stirred with a dream of the ultimate
    beauty,
A sense of the ultimate music,
I never shall capture;—

They are Beauty,
Formless and tremulous Beauty,

Beauty unborn;
Beauty as yet unappareled
In thought;
Beauty that hesitates,
Falters,
Withdraws from the verge of birth,
Flutters,
Retreats from the portals of life;—
O Beauty for ever uncaptured!
O songs that I never shall sing!

THE PARTING

We have come "the primrose way,"
  Folly, thou and I!
Such a glamor and a grace
Ever glimmered on they face,
Ever such a witchery
Lit the laughing eyes of thee,
Could a fool like me withstand
Folly's feast and beckoning hand?
Drinking, how thy lips' caress
Spiced the cup of waywardness!
So we came "the primrose way,"
  Folly, thou and I!

But now, Folly, we must part,
  Folly, thou and I!
Shall one look with mirth or tears
Back on all his wastrel years,
Purposes dissolved in wine,
Pearls flung to the heedless swine?—

Idle days and nights of mirth,
Were they pleasures nothing worth?
Well, there's no gainsaying we
Squandered youth right merrily!
But now, Folly, we must part,
  Folly, thou and I!

AN OPEN FIRE

THESE logs with drama and with dream are rife,
For all their golden Summers and green Springs
Through leaf and root they sucked the forest's life,
Drank in its secret, deep, essential things,
Its midwood moods, its mystic runes,
Its breathing hushes stirred of faery wings,
Its August nights and April noons;
The garnered fervors of forgotten Junes
Flare forth again and waste away;
And in the sap that leaps and sings
We hear again the chant the cricket flings
Across the hawthorn-scented dusks of May.

REALITIES

REALITIES

WE are deceived by the shadow, we see not the
substance of things.
For the hills are less solid than thought; and
deeds are but vapors; and flesh
Is a mist thrown off and resumed by the soul, as
a world by a god.
Back of the transient appearance dwells in ineffable calm
The utter reality, ultimate truth; this seems and
that is.

THE STRUGGLE

I HAVE been down in a dark valley;
I have been groping through a deep gorge;
Far above, the lips of it were rimmed with moonlight,
And here and there the light lay on the dripping rocks
So that it seemed they dripped with moonlight, not with water;
So deep it was, that narrow gash among the hills,
That those great pines which fringed its edge
Seemed to me no larger than upthrust fingers
Silhouetted against the sky;
And at its top the vale was strait,
And the rays were slant
And reached but part way down the sides;
I could not see the moon itself;
I walked through darkness, and the valley's edge
Seemed almost level with the stars,
The stars that were like fireflies in the little trees.

It was the midnight of defeat;
I felt that I had failed;
I was mocked of the gods;
There was no way out of that gorge;
The paths led no whither
And I could not remember their beginnings;
I was doomed to wander evermore,
Thirsty, with the sound of mocking waters in
    mine ears,
Groping, with gleams of useless light
Splashed in ironic beauty on the rocks above.
And so I whined.

And then despair flashed into rage;
I leapt erect, and cried:
"*Could I but grasp my life as sculptors grasp the clay*
And knead and thrust it into shape again!—
If all the scorn of Heaven were but thrown
Into the focus of some creature I could clutch!—
If something tangible were but vouchsafed me
By the cold, far gods!—
If they but sent a Reason for the failure of my life
I'd answer it;
If they but sent a Fiend, I'd conquer it!—

But I reach out, and grasp the air,
I rage, and the brute rock echoes my words in mockery—
How can one fight the sliding moonlight on the cliffs?
You gods, coward gods,
Come down, I challenge you!—
You who set snares with roses and with passion,
You who make flesh beautiful and damn men through the flesh,
You who plump the purple grape and then put poison in the cup,
You who put serpents in your Edens,
You who gave me delight of my senses and broke me for it,
You who have mingled death with beauty,
You who have put into my blood the impulses for which you cursed me,
You who permitted my brain the doubts wherefore you damn me,
Behold, I doubt you, gods, no longer, but defy!—
I perish here?
Then I will be slain of a god!
You who have wrapped me in the scorn of your silence,
The divinity in this same dust you flout

Flames through the dust,
And dares,
And flings you back your scorn,—
Come, face to face, and slay me if you will,
But not until you've felt the weight
Of all betricked humanity's contempt
In one bold blow!—
Speak forth a Reason, and I will answer it,
Yes, to your faces I will answer it;
Come garmented in flesh and I will fight with you,
Yes, in your faces will I smite you, gods;
Coward gods and tricksters that set traps
In paradise!—
Far gods that hedge yourselves about with silence
And with distance;
That mock men from the unscalable escarpments of
your Heavens."

Thus I raved, being mad.
I had no sooner finished speaking than I felt
The darkness fluttered by approaching feet,
And the silence was burned through by trembling
flames of sound,
And I was 'ware that Something stood by me.

And with a shout I leapt and grasped that Being,
And the Thing grasped me.
We came to wrestling grips,
And back and forth we swayed,
Hand seeking throat, and crook'd knee seeking
To encrook unwary leg,
And spread toes grasping the uneven ground;
The strained breast muscles cracked and creaked,
The sweat ran in my eyes,
The plagued breath sobbed and whistled through
  my throat,
I tasted blood, and strangled, but still struggled
  on—
The stars above me danced in swarms like yellow
  bees,
The shaken moonlight writhed upon the rocks;—
But at the last I felt his breathing weaker grow,
The tense limbs grow less tense,
And with a bursting cry I bent his head right
  back,
Back, back, until
I heard his neck bones snap;
His spine crunched in my grip;
I flung him to the earth and knelt upon his breast

And listened till the fluttering pulse was stilled.
Man, god, or devil, I had wrenched the life from
him!

And lo—even as he died
The moonlight failed above the vale,—
And somehow, sure, I know not how!—
Between the rifted rocks the great Sun struck
A finger down the cliff, and that red beam
Lay sharp across the face of him that I had slain;
And in that light I read the answer of the silent
gods
Unto my cursed-out prayer,
For he that lay upon the ground was—I!
I understood the lesson then;
It was myself that lay there dead;
Yes, I had slain my Self.

THE REBEL

No doubt the ordered worlds speed on
  With purpose in their wings;
No doubt the ordered songs are sweet
  Each worthy angel sings;
And doubtless it is wise to heed
  The ordered words of Kings;

But how the heart leaps up to greet
  The headlong, rebel flight,
Whenas some reckless meteor
  Blazes across the night!
Some comet—Byron—Lucifer—
  Has dared to Be, and fight!

No doubt but it is safe to dwell
  Where ordered duties are;
No doubt the cherubs earn their wage
  Who wind each ticking star;

No doubt the system is quite right!—
  Sane, ordered, regular;

But how the rebel fires the soul
  Who dares the strong gods' ire!
Each Byron!—Shelley!—Lucifer!—
  And all the outcast choir
That chant when some Prometheus
  Leaps up to steal Jove's fire!

THE CHILD AND THE MILL

Better a pauper, penniless, asleep on the kindly
sod—
Better a gipsy, houseless, but near to the heart
of God,

That beats for ears not dulled by the clanking
wheels of care—
Better starvation and freedom, hope and the good
fresh air

Than death to the Something in him that was
born to laugh and dream,
That was kin to the idle lilies and the ripples of
the stream.

For out of the dreams of childhood, that careless
come and go,
The boy gains strength, unknowing, that the Man
will prove and know.

But these fools with their lies and their dollars,
    their mills and their bloody hands,
Who make a god of a wheel, who worship their
    whirring bands,

They are flinging the life of a people, raw, to the
    brute machines.
Dull-eyed, weary, and old—old in his early teens—

Stunted and stupid and twisted, marred in the
    mills of grief,
Can your factories fashion a Man of this thing—
    a Man and a Chief?

Dumb is the heart of him now, at the time when
    his heart should sing—
Wasters of body and brain, what race will the
    future bring?

What of the nation's nerve whenas swift crises
    come?
What of the brawn that should heave the guns on
    the beck of the drum?

Thieves of body and soul, who can neither think
nor feel,
Swine-eyed priests of little false gods of gold and
steel,

Bow to your obscene altars, worship your loud
mills then!
Feed to Moloch and Baal the brawn and brains
of men—

But silent and watchful and hidden forever over
all
The masters brood of those Mills that "grind
exceeding small."

And it needs no occult art nor magic to foreshow
That a people who sow defeat they will reap the
thing they sow.

"SIC TRANSIT GLORIA MUNDI"

CONQUERORS leonine, lordly,
  Princes and vaunting kings,
Ye are drunk with the sound of your braggart
      trumps—
  But lo! ye are little things!

Earth . . . it is charnel with monarchs!
  And the puffs of dust that start
Where your war steeds stamp with their ringing hoofs
  Were each some warrior's heart.

Peoples imperial, mighty,
  Masterful, challenging fate,
The tread of your cohorts shakes the hills—
  But lo! ye are not great!

Nations that swarm and murmur,
  Ye are moths that flutter and climb—
Ye are whirling gnats, ye are swirling bees,
  Tossed in the winds of time!

Earth that is flushed with glory,
  A marvelous world ye are!
But lo! in the midst of a million stars
  Ye are only one pale star!

A breath stirs the dark abysses. . . .
  The deeps below the deep
Are troubled and vexed . . . and a thousand worlds
  Fall on eternal sleep!

THE COMRADE

I

Hath not man at his noblest
An air of something more than man?—
A hint of grace immortal,
Born of his greatly daring to assist the gods
In conquering these shaggy wastes,
These desert worlds,
And planting life and order in these stars?—
So Woman at her best:
Her eyes are bright with visions and with dreams
That triumph over time;
Her plumed thought, wing for wing, is mate with
his.

II

The world rolls on from dream to dream,
And 'neath the vast impersonal revenges of its
going,

Crushed fools that cried defeat
Lie dead amid the dust they prophesied—
Ye doubters of man's larger destiny,
Ye that despair,
Look backward down the vistaed years,
And all is battle—and all victory!
Man fought, to be a man!
Through painful centuries the slow beast fought,
Blinded and baffled, fought to gain his soul;—
Wild, hairy, shag, and feared of shadows,
Yet the clouds
Made him strange signals that he puzzled o'er;—
Beast, child, and ape,
And yet the winds harped to him, and the sea
Rolled in upon his consciousness
Its tides of wonder and romance;—
Uncouth and caked with mire,
And yet the stars said something to him, and the
sun
Declared itself a god;—
The lagging cycles turned at last
The pictures into thought,
Thought flowered in soul;—
But, oh, the myriad weary years

Ere Caliban was Shakespeare's self
And Darwin's ape had Darwin's brain!—
The battling, battling, and the steep ascent,
The fight to hold the little gained,
The loss, the doubt, the shaken heart,
The stubborn, groping slow recovery!—
But looking backward toward the dim beginnings,
You that despair,
Hath he not climbed and conquered?
Look backward and all's Victory!
What coward looks forward and foresees defeat?

III

Who climbed beside him, and who fought
And suffered and was glad?
Is she a lesser thing than he,
Who stained the slopes with bloody feet, or stood
Beside him on some hard-won eminence of hope
Exulting as the bold dawn swept
A harper hand along the ringing hills?
Flesh of his flesh, and of his soul the soul,
Hath she not fought, hath she not climbed?

And how is she a lesser thing?—
Nay, if she ever was
'Twas we that made her so, who called her queen
But kept her slave.

IV

Had she not courage for the fight?
Hath she not courage for the years to come?
Hath she not courage who descends alone—
(How pitifully alone, except for Love!)
Where man's thought even falters that would
    follow,
Into the shadowy abyss
(Through vast and murmurous caverns dark with
    crowding dread
And terrible with hovering wings),
To battle there with Death?—to battle
There with Death, and wrest from him,
O Conqueror and Mother,
Life!

V

Hath she too long dwelt dream-bound in the world
    of love,

Unconscious of the sterner throes,
The more austere, impersonal, wide faith,
The urge that drives Christs to the cross
Not for the love of one beloved,
But for the love of all?
If so, she wakes!
Wakes and demands a share in all man's bolder
destinies,
The high, audacious ventures of the soul
That thinks to scale the bastioned slopes
And strike stark Chaos from his throne.
We still stand in the dawn of time.
Not meanly let us stand nor shaken with low
doubts!
For there beyond the verge and margin of gray cloud
The future thrills with promise
And the skies are tremulous with golden light;—
She too would share those victories,
Comrade, and more than comrade;—
New times, new needs confront us now;
We must evolve new powers
To battle with;—
We must go forward now together,
Or perchance we fail!

ENVOI

A LITTLE WHILE

A little while the tears and laughter,
The willow and the rose—
A little while, and what comes after
No man knows.

An hour to sing, to love and linger . . .
Then lutanist and lute
Will fall on silence, song and singer
Both be mute.

Our gods from our desires we fashion. . . .
Exalt our baffled lives,
And dream their vital bloom and passion
Still survives;

But, when we're done with mirth and weeping,
With myrtle, rue, and rose,
Shall Death take Life into his keeping? . . .
No man knows.

What heart hath not, through twilight places,
Sought for its dead again
To gild with love their pallid faces? . . .
Sought in vain! . . .

Still mounts the Dream on shining pinion . . .
Still broods the dull distrust . . .
Which shall have ultimate dominion,
Dream, or dust?

A little while with grief and laughter,
And then the day will close;
The shadows gather . . . what comes after
No man knows!

THE END

CPSIA information can be obtained at www.ICGtesting.com
232230LV00003B/15/P

9 781171 6762